I0818339

HOW TO FIGHT

THICH NHAT HANH

Parallax Press
PO Box 7355
Berkeley, CA 94707
parallax.org

Parallax Press is the publishing division of Plum Village
Community of Engaged Buddhism, Inc.

Cover and text design by Debbie Berne
Illustrations by Jason DeAntonis

Printed in Canada by Friesens on FSC-certified paper

Parallax Press's authorized representative in the EU and the
EEA is SAS PLUM VILLAGE AT HOME- Point UH
437 Chemin du Pey, Thenac, France
Email: europe@parallax.org

Hardcover edition ISBN: 978-1-967175-28-4
Paperback original ISBN: 978-1-941529-86-7
Ebook ISBN: 978-1-941529-87-4

Library of Congress Cataloging-in-Publication Data
available upon request.

1 2 3 4 5 FRIESENS 29 28 27 26 25

CONTENTS

Notes on Fighting 7

Practices for Peace and Reconciliation 97

NOTES ON FIGHTING

OPENING THE DOOR

Never in human history have we had so many means of communication—television, radio, telephone, fax, email, the Internet—yet we remain islands, with little real communication between us. When we cannot communicate, we suffer, and we spill our suffering on to other people. We can find ways to open the doors of communication again.

WHERE THE FIGHT BEGINS

When someone says something unkind to you, you may want to retaliate right away. That is where the fight begins. This habitual way of reacting creates a well-worn pathway in your brain. When you travel a neural pathway over and over again, it becomes a habit. Very often that pathway leads to anger, fear, or craving. One millisecond is enough for you to arrive at the same destination: anger and a desire to punish the person who has dared to make you suffer. The mind and the brain are plastic in nature. You can change your mind, your brain, and the way you think and feel. With practice, you can create new neural pathways that lead to understanding, compassion, love, and forgiveness. Mindfulness and insight can intervene, redirecting you down a new neural pathway.

A PAUSE

Suppose someone just said something unpleasant to you. Their words and the sound of their voice give you an unpleasant feeling. You believe they are trying to make you suffer. Of course you feel the desire to react, to say something back. You feel that if you can express your anger, if you can make them suffer, you will get relief. Most of us react in that way. But mindfulness can help us pause for a moment and become aware of the anger building up in us. Stopping gives us a chance to acknowledge and to transform our anger. When we feel anger, irritation, or indignation arising in us, we pause. We stop and come back to our breathing straight away. We do not say or do anything when we are inhabited by this kind of energy, so we don't escalate the conflict. We wait until we're calm again. Being able to pause is the greatest gift. It gives us the opportunity to bring more love and compassion into the world rather than more anger and suffering.

WHEN YOUR HOUSE IS ON FIRE

Usually when we are angry with someone we are more interested in fighting with them than in taking care of our own feelings. It's like someone whose house is on fire running after the person who has set fire to their house instead of going home to put out the flames. If we don't go home to take care of our anger, our whole house will burn down. But if we can pause for a moment, we have a chance to acknowledge our anger, embrace it, and look deeply to see its true roots. If we can take care of our own anger instead of focusing on the other person, we will get immediate relief. If we can pause, we see that our anger or fear may have been born from a wrong perception or may have its roots in the large seeds of anger or fear within us. When we realize this, it frees us from anger and fear. Practice embracing and looking deeply to see the real roots of your anger. When insight is born, you will be free.

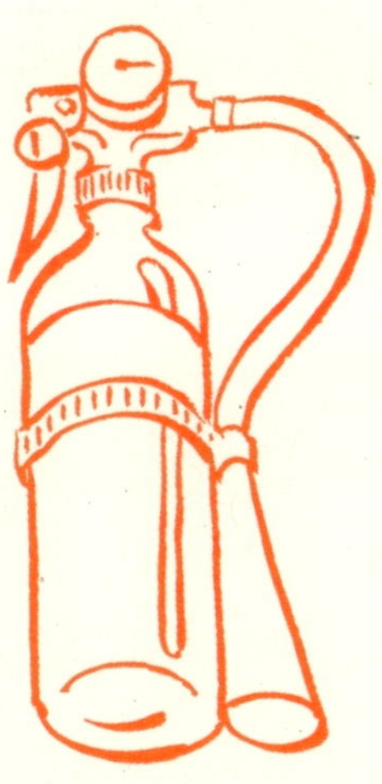

THE WARM AIR DOESN'T FIGHT THE COLD AIR

When it is cold in your room, you turn on the heater, and the heater begins to send out waves of hot air. The cold air doesn't have to leave the room for the room to become warm. The cold air is embraced by the hot air and becomes warm—there's no fighting at all between them. Mindfulness is the capacity to be aware of what is going on in the present moment. It is like warm air coming into a cold room. Mindfulness does not fight anger; it recognizes it and says hello. "Breathing in, I know that anger has manifested in me; breathing out, I smile to my anger." This is not an act of suppression or of fighting. It is an act of awareness. Once we recognize our anger, we can embrace it with tenderness.

DON'T RUN AWAY

To try to run away from suffering is not wise. To stay with it, to look deeply into it, and to make good use of it, is what we should do. It is by looking deeply into the nature of suffering that we discover the path of transformation and healing. Without suffering, there is no happiness and no path to happiness. We can even speak about the goodness of suffering because suffering helps us to learn and grow.

COUNTLESS OBSTACLES

Bodhisattvas are great beings who have dedicated their whole lives to cultivating compassion and liberating others from suffering. So is it possible for a bodhisattva to get angry? Of course it is. Being a bodhisattva doesn't mean you are perfect. Anyone who is aware of what is happening within themselves and tries to wake up other people is a bodhisattva. We are all bodhisattvas, doing our best. Along the way, we may feel angry or frustrated. It is said that when one bodhisattva gets angry at another bodhisattva, countless obstacles are set up everywhere in the universe. When we have hatred and anger in ourselves, they rebound to all quarters. When we have peace and joy in ourselves, our peace and joy will radiate throughout the whole cosmos.

KILLING ANGER

A Brahman asked the Buddha, "Master, is there anything you would agree to kill?" The Buddha answered, "Yes, anger. Killing anger removes suffering and brings peace and happiness." We "kill" our anger by smiling to it, holding it gently, looking deeply to understand its roots and transforming it with understanding and compassion. The Buddha's response so impressed the man, he became a monk. When his cousin learned of this, he cursed the Buddha to his face. The Buddha only smiled. The cousin became even more incensed and asked, "Why don't you respond?" The Buddha replied, "If someone refuses a gift, it must be taken back by the one who offered it." Angry words and actions hurt oneself first and hurt oneself most of all.

DON'T FIGHT WITH ANGER

Any peace talks should begin with making peace with ourselves. First we need to recognize our anger, embrace it, and make peace with it. You don't fight your anger, because your anger is you. Your anger is the wounded child in you. Why should you fight your anger? The method is entirely nonviolent: awareness, mindfulness, and tenderly holding your anger within you. Like this, your anger will transform naturally.

LISTENING TO OTHERS

We can only understand another person when we're able to truly listen to them. When we can listen to others with deep compassion, we can understand their pain and difficulties. But when we're angry, we can't listen to others or hear their suffering. Listening deeply to another is a form of meditation. We become aware of our breathing, follow it, and practice concentration, and we learn things about the other person that we never knew before. When we practice deep listening, we can help the person we're listening to remove the wrong perceptions that are making them suffer. We can restore harmony in our partnerships, our friendships, our family, our community, our nation, and between nations. It is that powerful.

LISTENING TO OURSELVES

Sometimes when we attempt to listen to another person, we can't hear them because we haven't listened to ourselves first. Our own strong emotions and thoughts are so loud in our heart and in our head, crying out for our attention, that we can't hear the other person. Before we listen to another, we need to spend time listening to ourselves. We can sit with ourselves, come home to ourselves, and listen to what emotions rise up, without judging or interrupting them. We can listen to whatever thoughts come up as well, and then let them pass without holding on to them. Then, when we've spent some time listening to ourselves, we are able to listen to those around us.

COMPASSIONATE LISTENING

When you practice compassionate listening, it's important to remember that you listen with only one aim, and that is to help the other person to suffer less. You give the other person a chance to say what is in their heart. Even if the other person says something harsh, provocative, or incorrect, or something full of blaming, judgement, or wrong perceptions, you still continue to listen with the heart of compassion. If you can maintain the energy of mindfulness and compassion in your heart while listening, you will be protected, and no matter what the other person says, it won't touch off the energy of irritation and anger in you. In that way, you can listen for an hour or more, and the quality of your listening will help the other person to suffer less. When people listen to each other like that, they truly recognize the humanity and the suffering of the other person. You see the other person is a human being, someone very much like yourself. You no longer look at that person with suspicion, anger, or fear.

LOVING SPEECH

Compassionate listening and loving speech are doors that can help us out of even the most difficult situations. Once we have listened with compassion, we can use loving speech to restore communication and understanding. We will know what to say and what not to say so we don't make the situation worse. To use loving speech means to speak in such a way that inspires joy, hope, and confidence in the other person. Our words water the wholesome seeds in us and in the other person. There is no anger, judgment, or blaming. We practice to calm ourselves before we express what is in our heart, and we choose our words carefully so the other person can accept what we say and can understand us better. We can practice loving speech every time we speak. Often our anger and irritation prevent us from being able to use loving speech, yet we know that if we speak with the energy of anger it will harm our relationship. Loving speech is an essential skill in building a relationship or a community that is a safe and healing refuge for all.

THE POWER OF GENTLENESS

Gentleness is powerful. When we use gentle and loving speech, we are able to transform all the anger, fear, resentment, and suspicion in our communication. The whole intention of loving speech is to understand the other person and to be understood.

GENEROSITY

Loving speech is an act of generosity. When we are motivated by loving kindness, we can bring happiness to many others through our kind words and actions. When we have a lot of pain, it is difficult to speak lovingly, so it is important to look deeply to see the roots of our anger, despair, and suffering, so we can understand and free ourselves from them. If we use words that inspire self-confidence, hope, and trust, especially with our children, they will flower.

ANGER IN THE LIVING ROOM

Using loving speech isn't easy. It takes diligence. This means first of all that we practice not watering the unbeneficial seeds in ourselves. In Buddhism, we speak of all the various potential states of mind as seeds. All of us have all of the seeds within us. We aren't necessarily aware of these seeds, but they are there in the lower level of our consciousness. The seeds contain the potential for all the different emotions, thoughts, and perceptions we may have. If something triggers one of the seeds—for example if someone says something unkind that waters your seed of anger—the seed of anger will come up and manifest in the upper level of consciousness, our mind. Loving speech requires that we notice when we're watering unwholesome seeds such as envy, anger, discrimination, or despair. Mindfulness of breathing or practicing mindful walking can be a soothing lullaby that helps us embrace the unwholesome seed with our awareness and invite it to go back to sleep. The lower level of consciousness is like the basement and the mind is the living room. If you allow anger to come up from the basement, it will occupy the whole living room. And if you allow anger to stay there for a long time, then the seed of anger will be strengthened in the lower level of consciousness. It will become more important and will arise more easily. If you get angry every day, your seed of anger will grow bigger and bigger, and it will be much more difficult for compassion to grow. Without compassion, it will be difficult to use loving speech.

RIGHT THINKING

If we want to avoid conflict and practice loving speech, we have to practice clear thinking. We will inevitably speak and act according to the way that we think. When we find ourselves thinking negatively about another person, rather than focusing on our negative thoughts and judgments, we can become interested in why they are the way they are. We can give our attention to the difficulties and hardships that person has had to face. We can bring to mind their positive qualities, good intentions, and kindness toward others, in order to give rise to our compassion and let go of our anger.

LOVE YOUR ENEMY

When we look deeply into our anger, we can see that the person we call our "enemy" is also suffering. Because they suffer so much, their suffering spills over on to us and on to others. When we recognize someone is suffering, it's easy to accept them and have compassion. This is what Jesus called "loving your enemy." Love means to embrace the other person with compassion. This is possible when we know the other person is suffering and needs our compassion, not our anger. When we're able to love our enemy, that person is no longer our enemy. The idea of "enemy" vanishes and is replaced by the person who is suffering and needs our compassion. Sometimes it's very easy, easier than you may think. What's important is to practice looking deeply.

MAN IS NOT OUR ENEMY

The roots of discrimination, conflict, and war are not to be found outside us. They are within our own way of thinking and looking at the world. The real enemy is our ignorance, our attachment to views, and our wrong perceptions. With looking deeply and the practice of compassionate dialogue, we can transform misperceptions and anger into understanding and love, just as a gardener can transform compost to grow beautiful flowers and vegetables.

HOW TO TELL THE TRUTH

When we want to prove a point, we may be tempted to twist the truth or say something that is only partially true. We may exaggerate by intentionally making something out to be greater or more extreme than it is. We may add, embellish, or invent details to prove we are right. This kind of speech can lead to misunderstanding and distrust. We have to practice speaking the truth and speaking it skillfully. If we're not skillful, we may say something that we think is truthful but it might still make others suffer or despair. Just because we have observed or experienced something doesn't mean we should speak about it if doing so will make others suffer. When we see someone suffer because of something we have said, we might say, "Well, I was only telling the truth." It may have been the truth, but it may also have been unskillful and hurtful. Loving speech requires telling the truth in such a way that it benefits others, the world, and ourselves. When we tell the truth, we do so with compassion; we speak in such a way that the hearer can accept what we're saying.

THE ART OF APOLOGIZING

The ability to apologize sincerely and express regret for the unskillful things we say or do is an art. A true apology can relieve a great deal of suffering in the other person. Once we realize that we may have said or done something to make another suffer, we can find a way to apologize as soon as possible. If we can, we should apologize right away and not wait. We can talk to the other person directly, or if they're not there we can call them on the phone, or even send a note. There is no need to wait until the next time we meet. A straightforward apology can have a powerful effect. We can just say, "I am very sorry. I know I was unskillful. I was not mindful or understanding." We don't need to justify or explain what we said or did, we just apologize.

UNCONDITIONAL REGRET

When you express regret, do so unconditionally. Don't make excuses for having committed the mistake. You can say, "I wasn't mindful at the time. I know that kind of language can be hurtful. Please forgive me. I don't want to say such things in the future." Don't apologize for the sake of receiving a reciprocal apology from the other person. When someone else offers us an apology, accept it and offer understanding and forgiveness in return.

STILLNESS IS THE FOUNDATION OF UNDERSTANDING

When we observe or listen to other people, we often don't see them clearly or really hear what they're saying. We see and hear our projections and prejudices instead. We have wrong perceptions about others, which color what we see and hear. Even if a friend gives us a compliment, we find it difficult to receive their kind words. Most of the time, our mind, thoughts, and feelings aren't calm. They're like the water in a muddy lake, which can't reflect the sky because it's been churned up by a storm. If we're not calm, we can't listen deeply and understand. But when our mind is calm, we can see reality more clearly, like still water reflecting the trees, the clouds, and the blue sky. Stillness is the foundation of understanding and insight. Stillness is strength.

BREATHE BEFORE SPEAKING

When you feel upset or angry, it's important not to do or say anything. We need to calm down first. Don't speak or act with the energy of anger in you. Just come back to your body and your breathing. Breathe in and out mindfully, releasing the tension in your body and mind, or go for a walk until you are calm enough. Then ask your friend to clarify what they were saying. Check to see if you have understood correctly, if your perceptions were correct. This will prevent a lot of damage to your relationship.

TREE IN A STORM

Many people don't know how to handle their strong emotions. Our wrong perceptions can make us angry or fill us with despair. To see clearly, we must calm down. When we're overcome by strong emotions we're like a tree in a storm, with its top branches and leaves swaying in the wind. But the trunk of the tree is solid, stable, and deeply rooted in the earth. When we're caught in a storm of emotions, we can practice to be like the trunk of the tree. We don't stay up in the high branches. We go down to the trunk and become still, not carried away by our thinking and emotions. We don't say or do anything; we just focus all our attention on the rise and fall of our abdomen, our trunk. This protects us from speaking in anger and saying something we may regret.

ACTING OUT

Some people believe that suffering, anger, and despair are poisons and you have to get them out of your system. But they may be useful and can be transformed into something positive right there where they are. When you try to get anger out by hitting something like a pillow, it may seem harmless. But it's not certain that you can release your anger by hitting the pillow, imagining it to be your enemy, the one who has made you suffer. You may be rehearsing your anger and making it stronger instead of releasing it. It may seem safe to hit a pillow, because it's not a person or an animal. But doing this will water the seed of anger in your unconscious mind. By rehearsing our anger we are creating a habit of being angry, which can be dangerous and destructive.

FEEDING OUR SUFFERING

The Buddha said, "Nothing can survive without food"—not even love. Without nourishment, your love will die. You can learn ways to nourish your love every day, so that your love can continue to thrive. What kind of food are you feeding your love? When you produce loving thoughts, speech, and actions, these nourish your love and help it grow strong. Suffering also requires food to survive. If you continue to suffer, it's because you feed your suffering every day. Thoughts, conversations, films, books, magazines, and the Internet are sensory foods that we consume. If we don't carefully choose what we consume, these things can water the seeds of anger, fear, violence, and discrimination within us. If you stop feeding your suffering, it will also die.

THE USEFULNESS OF SUFFERING

The substance that can neutralize anger is compassion. If you know how to generate the energy of compassion, it can transform your anger. When you can see another person's suffering, when you have understood their suffering, suddenly compassion is born in you. When compassion is born, you don't suffer anymore when you look at the person who has harmed or hurt you. You no longer want to punish that person. Instead, you want to help them to suffer less. We can speak of the goodness of suffering. Suffering brings about understanding and compassion, which are the true foundations of happiness.

NO MUD NO LOTUS

Transforming our anger and suffering makes happiness possible. Without suffering there can be no happiness. We need mud to grow lotus flowers, otherwise they cannot take root. Our anger and suffering are the mud we can use to cultivate happiness, compassion, and understanding. If we know how to handle and transform our suffering, we will suffer much less. The mud will become lotus flowers. To generate compassion, you have to understand and embrace your own suffering. Don't try to throw your suffering away. Hold it tenderly like a mother holding her crying baby, and look deeply into it. Then insight can bloom. Each person has a lot of anger and suffering inside. When we don't know how to handle our suffering, we continue to suffer, and we can make other people around us suffer. When someone hurts us, our first reaction is to want to punish or hurt them. But when we understand that others are already suffering, we don't want to punish them anymore. Listening to the suffering inside of you and inside of the other person allows understanding and compassion to be born. When compassion is born in your heart, it begins to heal and transform the anger and suffering in your heart and in every cell of your body.

LOOKING AT OTHERS

When you're sitting on a bus or in the subway, instead of thinking of this and that, look at the people around you. Looking deeply at the expressions on their faces, you will see their suffering. When you touch suffering like that, compassion is born in you. Looking at living beings through the eyes of compassion is a very strong practice. A week of practice like that can make a big difference in your life and in the lives of others.

THE FIVE-YEAR-OLD CHILD

Often, our suffering begins when we are quite young and continues to fester as we grow. There is a five-year-old still inside us. This child may have suffered a lot. A five-year-old is fragile and easily wounded. Without mindfulness parents may transmit all their pain, anger, and suffering to their children. By the age of five, the child is already filled with fear and sorrow. A child so young isn't always able to explain her suffering in a way that others can hear. As she stumbles over her words, adults around her might interrupt or even shout at her. Such language is like ice water thrown over a tender heart. The child may never try to confide in grown-ups again, and the wound remains deep and hidden. Adults repeat acts like this over and over until their connection with their children is severed. The cause is a lack of mindfulness. If a parent doesn't know how to manage his anger, for example, he may destroy the communication with his child and the child may suffer their whole life, and pass that anger on to the next generation. So it is important to get in touch with the five-year-old child within, and begin to heal the wounds still inside. We can learn to listen to the suffering of our five-year-old, to embrace it tenderly. Holding our pain and suffering with the energy of mindfulness and compassion, it begins to transform.

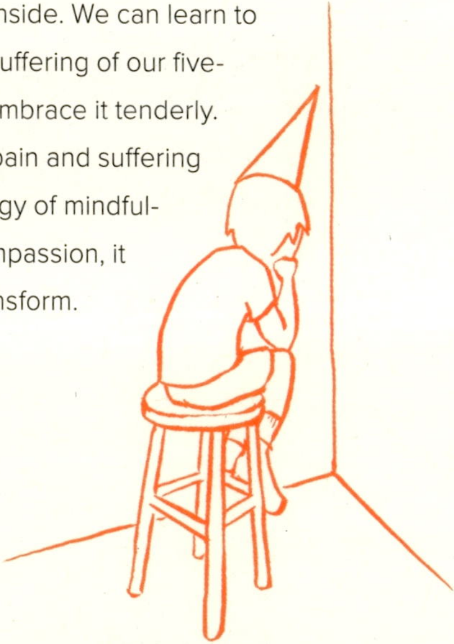

PEACE IN ONESELF

We can only listen to another person and understand their suffering if we have first looked deeply, embraced, and been kind to our own fear and anger. We make peace with our own fears, worries, and resentments and look deeply to understand their roots. This brings the insight that can transform and heal. The process of going home and making peace inside is critical to being able to offer love to another person. Everyone knows that peace must begin with oneself, but not everyone knows how to do it. With the practice of mindful breathing, calming the mind and relaxing the body, you can start making peace inside you, and you'll feel much better right away. Before you do the work of reconciliation with another, you need to restore communication with yourself.

MAKING PEACE

Mindful breathing is a wonderful way to help you make peace with yourself. Simply by bringing your full awareness to your in-breath and your out-breath, you slow down. While you practice mindful breathing, you become present. You do not have to know what to say or do. Whatever else is going on, you can take a moment to simply notice,

> Breathing in,
> I am aware I am breathing in.
>
> Breathing out,
> I am aware I am breathing out.

Breathing with awareness, peace comes naturally. The energy of mindfulness has the elements of attentiveness, concern, and friendship in it. Just by practicing awareness of your breathing, the person you are having difficulty with may notice there is a change taking place in you. Although you have not yet reopened communication or started the process of making peace with the other person, your peaceful energy has already had an effect on them. When we are aware of our breathing in and out, we are on the path to becoming more mindful, and mindfulness is the beginning of awakening.

THE LANGUAGE OF LOVE

We need to reconcile within ourselves before we can reconcile with someone else. We recognize and embrace all our feelings and emotions. We see that the cause of our suffering lies within us and not in the other person—they have only touched the seed of suffering already inside us. Understanding this, we can see our own part in the difficulty that has arisen, and compassion can be born.

When you have reconciled and are at peace with yourself, it is much easier to go to the other person and say, "I know you have suffered a lot. I know I have also contributed to your suffering. I haven't been very mindful or skillful. I didn't understand your suffering and difficulties enough. I may have said or done things that have made the situation worse. I'm sorry. I didn't mean to hurt you. Your happiness, your safety, your freedom, and your joy are important to me. Because I have been caught in my own suffering, I have been unskillful at times. I may have given you the impression that I wanted to make you suffer. That's not true. So please tell me about your suffering so that I will not make the same kind of mistake again. I know that your happiness is crucial to my own happiness. I need your help. Tell me about your fear and despair, your difficulties, your dreams, so that I can understand you better."

VICTIM NUMBER TWO

Suppose someone has made you suffer a lot. You may believe that you are the only one who suffers and that the other person is thoughtless or vindictive and that's why they made you suffer. But if you have the time and patience to look deeply, you will recognize the suffering in the other person. Because that person does not know how to handle their own suffering, they remain the first and biggest victim of their suffering. You are only victim number two.

HOW CAN I HELP?

Sometimes you believe that you are doing something out of love and in the service of another person's happiness. But if you don't act from a place of deep understanding of the other person, your actions may actually be making them suffer. If you don't understand the suffering, the difficulties, and the deep aspirations of another person, it's not possible for you to love them. Love is understanding; without understanding we cannot speak of true love. A person should be able to ask another person: "Do I understand you well enough?" That is the language of love. If you are sincere, the other person will tell you about their suffering. When you have understood their suffering, you can provide the food of love.

NOWHERE IS TOO FAR AWAY

Sometimes, the person we want to reconcile with is far away and we feel we have lost the chance to mend our relationship. Why not use a phone? If the other person can hear your voice, it helps avoid misperceptions. So it's better not to rely on texting or email to heal your relationship. Do not worry too much about the words. As long as you are practicing mindful breathing and have made peace with yourself, the other person will hear that in your voice. If you are solid and at peace with yourself, your words will open the door to the heart of the other person. It might not happen right away, but the door will eventually crack open.

RECONCILING WITH THOSE WHO HAVE DIED

Do you regret not having said the right thing to someone before they died? Do you regret something you did during their lifetime, and now you feel it's too late? You don't need to feel regret, because that person is still in you. There's no need to feel guilt. Everything is still possible. The past is not gone; it is still available in the form of the present. If we know how to touch the present deeply, we can touch the past, and even transform it. Smile to the one who has died and say the things you wish you had said but didn't have a chance to. Express your love and your gratitude. That will bring you peace and will renew your relationship. It will also bring joy to the people around you and to future generations.

WHAT WILL MAKE US SAFE?

Very often in a conflict, we believe the problem is the other person or group. We think it is all their fault and that if they would just stop doing what they are doing or being the way they are, we would have peace and happiness. So we may be motivated by the desire to destroy the other side. We may wish they didn't exist. But looking deeply, we know that we are not the only ones who have suffered—they have also suffered. When we take time to calm ourselves down and look deeply into the situation, we can see that we are co-responsible, that we have co-created the conflict by our way of thinking, acting, or speaking, either individually or as a group or nation. We can look deeply to see our own part in the difficulty that has arisen and accept responsibility. When we see how we have contributed to the conflict, our heart opens again and dialogue becomes possible. We want to create the opportunity for ourselves to live in peace, in safety, in security, and also for the other side to live in peace, safety, and security. If you have this intention and you know how to include the other side in your heart, then you suffer less right away. The other side also wants to live in safety and peace. When we are motivated and animated by the desire to include, it's very easy to ask the other side: "How can we best ensure our mutual safety and happiness?" When we are able to ask that question, the situation can change on a deep level very quickly.

ARE YOU SURE?

Many arguments and conflicts come about because we are so sure of our own thoughts and perceptions. One of the deepest teachings given by the Buddha is that we should not be too sure of our own ideas. Don't be fooled by your perceptions. Even if you are sure you are seeing clearly, check again. Keep an open mind. Be ready to let go of your views. The same applies to how we see each other and the world. Have we understood the situation clearly? We have a responsibility to reflect the situation accurately, not colored by the lens of our fear or our discriminating mind. Clear, unbiased observation and loving speech can contribute greatly to building connection and removing anger, hatred, and discrimination.

WRONG PERCEPTIONS

Sometimes we have the impression that someone intentionally wants to make us suffer. Believing this, we get very angry, even despairing, and we want to hurt that person in return, firmly convinced they are a threat to us. War is a product of this kind of misunderstanding and of fear on a large scale. We can see the same thing in our own lives on a smaller scale. When communication is not good, it's easy to have wrong perceptions. One way to remove these wrong perceptions is to establish a dialogue. We can say, "I want to make sure that I understand what you are saying." Questioning our perceptions and listening deeply without prejudice or judgment is a very strong practice.

AN OPEN MIND

Often we not only have wrong perceptions about others, we also have wrong perceptions about ourselves. Before beginning a dialogue with someone, it's important to practice conscious breathing. Calming our emotions and looking deeply, we can become aware of our feelings and of whatever misperceptions we might have that could prevent us from hearing and understanding the other person. This will make our communication with others much more successful. Practicing in this way, you are doing your best to see and hear clearly, so that what you perceive will not be the creation of your subjective mind. With a mind that is calm and free from preconceived ideas, you are able to be in touch with reality.

HOW LARGE IS YOUR HEART?

The practice of inclusiveness is based on the practice of understanding, compassion, and love. With understanding and love you can embrace and accept everything, and everyone, and you don't have to suffer, because your heart is large. How can we enlarge our heart? Increasing our understanding and compassion makes our heart grow greater. Each of us has to ask the question: is there anything that we can do to help us open the door of our heart and accept the other person? How large is our heart?

INTERNAL KNOTS

In Buddhist psychology, we find the term "internal formations" or "internal knots." When someone says something unkind to us and we don't understand why, we may become upset. A knot is tied inside us. Lack of understanding is the basis for every internal knot. It's difficult for us to accept that we have negative feelings like anger, fear, and regret. We create elaborate defense mechanisms to deny their existence, but these feelings are always trying to surface. We can learn the skill of recognizing a knot the moment it is tied in us, and we can find ways to untie it. If we give it our full attention as soon as it forms, while still loosely tied, untying it will be easy. Otherwise, it grows tighter and stronger with time and is more difficult to loosen.

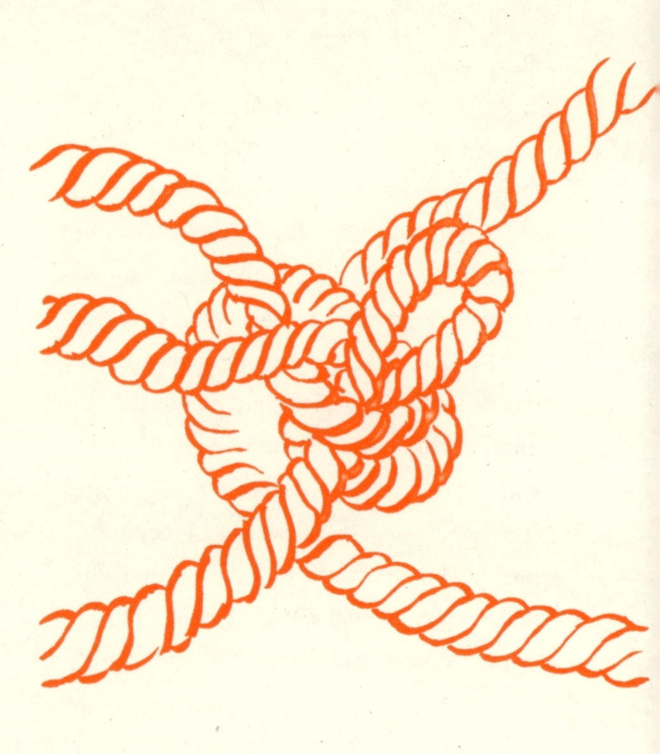

UNTYING KNOTS IN A RELATIONSHIP

When you are in a new relationship, both people are still light, and have few knots. Misunderstandings are easy to clear up right away. But when we let things build up, many knots accumulate and we don't know where to begin untying them. To protect each other's happiness, we need to become aware of and communicate about our internal knots as soon as they arise. One woman told me that just three days after her wedding she already had a number of knots inside but she kept them from her partner for thirty years. She was afraid that if she told him, there would be a fight. We can't be truly happy without real, open communication. When we are not mindful in our daily life, we plant seeds of suffering in the very person we love the most.

GIVE A GIFT

When we're angry with someone, and we've tried many ways but have still not been able to resolve the difficulty, we can try offering the other person a gift. We prepare the gift in advance, when we're happy, calm, and solid, and we hide it, ready for the time when we may need it. We don't wait until we're already angry because then we won't feel like doing it. Then, when we're angry, we can get it out of hiding and give it to the other person. This brings immediate relief. Usually, when we fight, we just want to punish the other person. But by doing the opposite, by giving them something they like, our anger dies down, and very quickly we arrive at the shore of love and understanding.

INTERBEING

Interbeing is the understanding that nothing exists separately from anything else. We are all interconnected. By taking care of another person, you take care of yourself. By taking care of yourself, you take care of the other person. Happiness and safety are not individual matters. If you suffer, I suffer. If you are not safe, I am not safe. There is no way for me to be truly happy if you are suffering. If you can smile, I can smile too. The understanding of interbeing is very important. It helps us to remove the illusion of loneliness, and transform the anger that comes from the feeling of separation.

HOW TO DEFUSE A BOMB

When you contain too much violence and anger within yourself, you become so tense that you are like a bomb about to go off. You suffer very much, and your suffering spills out all over the people you live or work with. People become afraid of you, they don't want to approach you. So you believe that everyone is boycotting you. You become extremely lonely. When we suffer, we have the tendency to blame other people and to see them as the source of our suffering. We don't recognize that we are responsible to some extent for our suffering as well as for making those around us suffer. We don't see that while others may want to help us, we have become like a bomb, ready to explode. Or perhaps you know someone like that, and although you would like to reach out to them, you feel they might explode at any moment so you keep your distance. You have to train yourself first to become skillful. Practice mindful breathing, mindful walking, embracing your own suffering, and using loving speech. Then, you can approach the other person with your solid presence and your mindful speech. This can be very healing for both people. With deep listening and loving speech, you may be able to restore communication.

THREE SENTENCES FOR WHEN YOU ARE SUFFERING

These three sentences can help when you are angry and do not want to be carried away by your anger.

The first line is, "Breathing in, I know I'm suffering." We often don't realize when we are suffering, and so we become a victim of our suffering. By saying, "Breathing in, I know I'm suffering," there is suffering but there is also mindfulness of suffering. That makes a big difference.

The second line is, "I know that you are suffering too." Usually we think that we are the only one who is suffering, that we are the victim of the unkindness or cruelty of the other person. We forget that the other person is also suffering, and that is why they said or did such things.

The third line is, "I need your help." We need help because we are suffering. We want to understand what has happened. The other person also needs our help, not punishment. This simple phrase can remind us that we can offer to be a refuge for each other rather than making things worse. We can de-escalate tension and conflict straight away by asking the other person for help.

BETRAYAL AND FAITHFULNESS

Where there is betrayal, there is also faithfulness. Everyone has both the seed of betrayal and the seed of faithfulness. No situation between two people is ever just one person's responsibility. If you are in a relationship, you can water the seed of faithfulness in yourself and in your partner every day. The way you speak, look, and act can be full of compassion and loving kindness. When someone is compassionate, people naturally like to come and sit close to them, the way people like to sit and relax at the foot of a big, shady tree. If we can stay fresh, compassionate, loving, and patient, we can help transform our relationship and the other person.

USE YOUR COMMUNITY

Part of acknowledging suffering is acknowledging we need help. It is much easier to practice compassion if you have the energy and support of a community. A community helps us not lose hope. It's not always easy to resolve our suffering alone. We're all unskillful at times. Even if we don't want to harm anyone or create suffering, we do it anyway. We can't be skillful all the time. Every one of us needs help. Find a way to be with others who know how to look and listen deeply, who can help us understand the situation more clearly. This will nourish your compassion. With compassion in our heart we suffer less, because compassion has the power to heal. Take refuge in a community, and then you will be able to help others as you help yourself.

SKILLFULNESS

Learn to nourish yourself and your loved ones with joy. To love someone means to understand them. It means knowing how to bring them joy and happiness in concrete ways. If you act skillfully, your words and actions will make the other person feel fresh and light. Sometimes a kind word or two are enough to help them blossom like a flower. We have to learn the art of creating happiness. If during our childhood we saw our mother or father do things that created happiness in the family, we will already know how to do this. But if our parents did not know how to create happiness, we may not know how to do it either. In our practice community, we try to learn the art of making people happy. The problem is not one of being wrong or right, but one of being more or less skillful. Creating happiness is an art. Living together is an art. Even with a lot of goodwill, you can still make the other person very unhappy. Goodwill is not enough. We need to know the art of making the other person happy. Art is the essence of life. Try to be artful in your speech and actions. The substance of art is mindfulness. When you are mindful, you are more artful. This is something I have learned from the practice.

A COUNCIL OF SAGES

There are people who feel they have never been truly seen or listened to by others. Suffering is there. We have to practice listening to the pain of other people. There are people who have the capacity to listen deeply with compassion to suffering. We should be able to look around, identify them, and invite them to form a commission for deep listening, a kind of council of sages, in order to practice listening to the suffering of our own nation and people. A person needs to act compassionately within her own frontiers first, before one can think of helping others. Acting with compassion and wisdom within our own frontiers is the first step to helping the world.

INTERNATIONAL RECONCILIATION

One person's suffering represents the suffering of the world. If you can help one person, you help the whole world. Unless we've been able to listen to our own fear and anger, we won't be able to listen to and understand the fear and anger of other nations and people. Hatred, violence, anger, and terrorism are born from wrong perceptions. As nations and individuals, we have so many wrong perceptions about ourselves and about each other, and these are the foundation of our hatred, fear, and distrust. Each one of us needs to practice looking and listening deeply so we can understand ourselves and others and the situation better and remove our wrong perceptions. This work cannot be achieved with bombs, guns, or military might. Nor can it be done by our elected leaders. The situation of our country and our world is too important to be entrusted to politicians alone. We need to practice deep, compassionate listening and loving speech with ourselves, with our loved ones, with our community, with strangers, and at all levels of society.

A FRESH BEGINNING

Of course we have made mistakes. Of course we have not been very skillful. Of course we have made ourselves and the people around us suffer. But that does not prevent us from improving, from transforming, from beginning anew. To begin anew is to look deeply and honestly at ourselves, our past actions, speech, and thoughts, and to create a fresh beginning within ourselves and in our relationships with others. The Buddha said that if you have not suffered, there is no way you can learn. We learn by making mistakes. We can begin anew at the last moment of the day and even at the last moment of our life. In one day, in twenty-four hours, you have hundreds of chances to begin anew.

UNILATERAL DISARMAMENT

When you have reconciled internally, peace and love become possible. When you embody peace and love, you can change a difficult situation more easily. Disarmament can be done unilaterally. If you disarm yourself, it means you've decided not to attack or inflict injury; you have become peaceful. Even if the other person is not aware of it yet, the moment you disarm yourself, give up the fight, and practice beginning anew in yourself, healing begins and you undergo a transformation that very soon will have an effect on the other person. They may then also decide to disarm and succeed in transforming their wrong perceptions, anger, and violence, too. We can do this as individuals and also as a nation.

TAKING CARE OF ONESELF IS TAKING CARE OF EACH OTHER

The Buddha told a story of an acrobatic master and his pupil. They went to the market every day to give a performance. The man held a bamboo pole, and the little girl climbed very high up the bamboo pole. One day the master said, "My child, let us take good care of each other. I'll take care of you and you take care of me, and that way we can both be safe and stay alive while we perform and earn our living." The young girl replied, "But master, I see it differently. I think that if I take good care of myself and you take good care of yourself then we'll both be safe, able to support each other, and to continue making a living." The little girl understood the true nature of interbeing. There is no discrimination, no separation. When you take good care of yourself, you are taking care of the other person. Looking after ourselves means looking after others. How do we look after ourselves? By practicing mindfulness. By knowing what is going on in our body and mind. We bring our mind home to our body and establish ourselves firmly in the present moment. We bring our awareness to our breathing and relax our body. Taking care of our strong emotions and learning to recognize our wrong perceptions, we discover the roots of our suffering. How do we take care of others? When you go to work, drive carefully—that's the way to take care of your daughter, your son, your partner. You will amaze yourself. You will find that by taking care of yourself, by healing the wounds in yourself, you begin to heal the wounds in the other person. The other person will be able to see your transformation.

IMPERMANENCE

There is a tendency to believe that we will remain the same person forever, and that the person we are fighting with will remain the same person forever, that they will never change. This kind of delusion prevents us from living in a way that can bring happiness to ourself and to the other person. Usually, when we lose something or someone, we begin to suffer. But while that something or some-one is still there, we don't appreciate them. Everything is of the nature to change. When we understand this, we appreciate the other person more deeply and we can do something today to make them happy, because we know tomorrow may be too late.

DEALING WITH CONFUSION

There are moments when we feel lost, we feel confused, we don't know what is the right thing to do. To fight back or not to fight back? To say something or not? To leave or to stay? We are confused. The best thing to do in that moment is to stop and go home to yourself with mindful breathing. Bringing awareness to our breathing, we calm down and have more clarity. In a state of confusion, fear can be born, and we may do things that make the situation worse. So the right thing to do is not to do anything. Just go home to yourself and practice mindful breathing in order to be your best. Because if you have enough tranquility, calm, and peace, the insight will come as to what is the best thing to say or do to help the situation.

PREVENT THE NEXT WAR

Only if you suffer will you make other people suffer. If you are peaceful and happy, you won't inflict suffering on other people. Looking deeply we can see how we have helped create the suffering in those who inflict violence, through our forgetfulness and through the way we live our daily lives. We have to learn to produce right thinking, speech, and action that is free of violence, anger, hate, and fear. We know very well that violence only creates more violence. Yet violence has become the substance of our lives. Many of us live in places where there is fighting in the streets and in our homes. Is it any wonder, then, that we fight and see violence as the way to solve problems? If we want to protect life, we have to look deeply as individuals and as a nation into the true nature of violence and war. We have to do everything in our power to prevent war from happening again. If we only protest, we will not be ready when the next war comes in five or ten years. To prevent the next war, we have to practice peace today. If we establish peace in our hearts, in our way of looking at things, and in our way of being with each other and with the world, then we are doing our best to make sure the next war will not come. War is the fruit of our collective consciousness. If we wait until another war is imminent to begin to practice peace, it will be too late. Peace begins here, now.

ONE ARROW CAN SAVE TWO BIRDS

When you remove the conflict within yourself, you also remove the conflict between yourself and others. One arrow can save two birds at the same time—if the arrow strikes the branch, both birds will fly away. First, take care of yourself. Reconcile the conflicting elements within yourself by being mindful, looking deeply, and practicing loving kindness and compassion toward yourself. Then, reconcile with the people closest to you by understanding and loving them, even if they themselves sometimes lack understanding.

HEALING

When we become aware that we've done something to cause others to be unhappy, what can we do? The people we have made suffer may still be alive or may already have died. What can we do to make amends? The wound is not only in the body and consciousness of the other person, but the wound is also there in you. The pain, the suffering, is still there in your consciousness. When you become aware of the wound, you can begin to breathe in and out and say, "Breathing in, I am aware of the wound in me; breathing out, I am taking good care of the wound in me." Breathing in, I say "I am sorry," breathing out, "I will not do that again."

WHERE WILL WE BE

Being angry in the historical dimension
I close my eyes and look deeply:
Three hundred years from now
where will you be and where shall I be?

PRACTICES FOR PEACE AND RECONCILIATION

AWARENESS OF SORROW

Breathing mindfully, you generate the energy of mindfulness that you can use to recognize and embrace your pain and sorrow. This brings relief and joy, diminishes pain, and transforms suffering. We do not try to run away from our difficult feelings and emotions. Breathing mindfully, we embrace them. Mindful breathing calms and purifies body and mind. It helps us let go of any tension in the body, and of any worries we may have about the past or the future. Mindful breathing helps us see reality as it is, and helps us let go of our wrong views and afflictions. Breathing mindfully relieves suffering and restores balance and happiness. The practice of mindful breathing can bring well-being, solidity, and freedom.

DEEP LISTENING PRACTICE

Deep listening is the basis for reconciliation. Whenever we want to practice the art of deep listening, we can first recite this verse. Avalokiteshvara is a great being who has the capacity to listen deeply to relieve suffering.

> We invoke your name, Avalokiteshvara. We aspire to learn your way of listening in order to help relieve the suffering in the world. You know how to listen in order to understand. We invoke your name in order to practice listening with all our attention and openheartedness. We will sit and listen without any prejudice. We will sit and listen without judging or reacting. We will sit and listen in order to understand. We will sit and listen so attentively that we will be able to hear what the other person is saying and also what is being left unsaid. We know that just by listening deeply we already alleviate a great deal of pain and suffering in the other person.

BELLY BREATHING TO CALM STRONG EMOTIONS

Sometimes we can feel overwhelmed by our emotions, and we forget we are much more than our emotions. When a strong emotion comes up, we can say, "Hello, my emotion. I know you are there. I will take care of you." Practice mindful, deep, abdominal breathing. Sit down or lie down. Put your hand on your abdomen, just below the navel, and breathe in very deeply, breathe out very deeply. Become aware of the rising and falling of your belly. Stop all thinking, just focus on your breath and your abdomen.

Breathing in,
my abdomen is rising.
Breathing out,
my abdomen is falling.

The more you think about what has upset you, the stronger your emotion will become. So keep bringing your awareness back to your breath as it goes down into the abdomen and out again. Feel the abdomen rising and falling as the air goes in and out. Know that you can handle the storm in you. You are much more than one emotion.

THE SIX MANTRAS

A mantra is a magic formula that, when recited with concentration and insight, has the power to change the situation. For it to work, we need to be fully present when we pronounce it. Sometimes we say the mantras out loud for the other person to hear and sometimes we say them quietly to ourselves. You can say just the one that works for you or rewrite them to fit your own needs.

1. I AM HERE FOR YOU

Sometimes we hide ourselves in the morning news at breakfast time. Sometimes we're lost in our thinking and our plans. We're driving our car and our loved one is sitting beside us but we have forgotten all about her. Sometimes we're eating a meal and we don't even know who's there eating with us. Our loved one is there physically but it's as if she's not truly there. To love someone, you need to be there one hundred percent. The mantra "I am here for you" says that I care about you, I enjoy being in your presence. It helps the other person to feel supported and happy.

2. I KNOW YOU ARE THERE AND I AM VERY HAPPY

Sometimes we forget about impermanence. We think that our loved one will be with us forever and we forget how precious her presence is in this moment. Once we're really there for the other person, that person becomes something very real. When the other person is real, she is a wonderful manifestation of life and we need to let her know that, for her happiness and for our own.

3. I FEEL YOUR PAIN AND I AM HERE FOR YOU

We may have said or done something to hurt another person. If we have hurt that person, we need to know about it. But don't expect the other person to be able to talk about it straight away. It may still be too painful. But you do want the other person to know that you are sensitive to his pain and that you're ready just to sit, breathe, and be with that person. Acknowledging the other person's suffering and offering your support already brings relief.

4. I AM SUFFERING; PLEASE HELP

Sometimes this mantra is the most difficult one to practice. It takes humility to admit that you have been hurt and need help; our pride or fear of rejection may get in the way. Still, we have to let our loved ones know when they've hurt us, otherwise many hurts can accumulate until we can't bear it anymore and want to separate from each other. This mantra could mean: "Please be there to listen to what hurt me, and please explain to me why you said or did such a thing."

5. THIS IS A HAPPY MOMENT

This mantra can be practiced at any moment. We have the tendency to forget the many conditions for happiness that are already available to us. We can remember this, and remind each other, by saying this mantra. So when you sit down to a meal together, someone can ask: "What kind of moment is this?" And the other can reply: "This is a happy moment."

6. YOU ARE PARTLY RIGHT

Sometimes we receive a large amount of praise. We do need to be praised from time to time, but we want to be careful not to become too proud because of the praise. So you say to yourself or aloud: "You are partly right." It means: "Yes, I do have that gift but it's not just mine; it has been handed down to me by my ancestors. And everyone has talents and gifts of some kind."

Sometimes we are criticized. We do need a certain amount of feedback in order to help us progress, but it's important not to be caught in the criticism and become paralyzed by it. You can say the mantra to yourself or out loud, "You are partly right." It means: "Yes, I do manifest that unfortunate characteristic sometimes, but I am much more than that. This is something that I have received from my ancestors and I am in the process of transforming it, for their sake and for mine."

MEDITATION ON THE FIVE-YEAR-OLD CHILD

A five-year-old child is vulnerable and can get hurt very easily. We have all been a five-year-old, and that child is still alive inside us. In this meditation, you go home and touch the five-year-old child in you, the child who may be deeply wounded and who has been neglected for a long time. Sitting and breathing, perhaps looking at a photo of yourself at age five, you can say, "Seeing myself as a five-year-old child, I breathe in. Smiling to the five-year-old child, I breathe out."

The next step is to imagine the person who you perceive as causing your suffering as a five-year-old child. It can be helpful to imagine your parents as five-year-old children. You can say, "Breathing in, I see my father as a five-year-old child. Breathing out, I smile to the five-year-old child that was my father." We may have an image of our father as an adult, but we forget that he was once a little boy whose feelings were also easily hurt. If it helps, find a photo of your father as a small child and look at it. Breathe in and out and smile at your father as a five-year-old child. You will see that your father carries wounds in himself just like you do. In that moment, you *are* your father. You become one with the object of your contemplation, and understanding and compassion can arise.

You might like to practice the following guided sitting meditation:

> Seeing myself as a five-year-old child,
> I breathe in.
> Smiling to the five-year-old child, I breathe out.
>
> Seeing the five-year-old as fragile and
> vulnerable, I breathe in.

Smiling with love to the five-year-old in me,
I breathe out.

Seeing my father as a five-year-old boy,
I breathe in.
Smiling to my father as a five-year-old boy,
I breathe out.

Seeing my five-year-old father as fragile and vulnerable, I breathe in.
Smiling with love and understanding to my father as a five-year-old boy, I breathe out.

Seeing my father suffering as a child,
I breathe in.
Seeing my mother suffering as a child,
I breathe out.

Seeing my father and mother in me,
I breathe in.
Smiling to my father and mother in me,
I breathe out.

BEGINNING ANEW

Beginning Anew is a practice to help resolve conflict or a difficulty when it arises. To begin anew is to look honestly at ourselves, at what we have thought, said, or done that has contributed to the conflict. This can help prevent feelings of hurt from building up and defuse difficult situations. It is a practice of recognition and appreciation of the positive elements within ourselves and the other person.

First we begin anew for ourselves and then we can begin anew with the other person. We can practice beginning anew with our partner, parents, children, friends, or coworkers.

The practice has four stages: "flower watering" (expressing our appreciation), expressing regrets, expressing hurts, and asking for support.

1. FLOWER WATERING

We look deeply to see the positive qualities in the other person and express our appreciation for them. Share at least three positive qualities that you have observed in them and things for which you feel grateful. Be as concrete as possible. Sometimes we may need to water someone's flowers for a long time to heal the relationship and build trust before we can express what has hurt us. This is an opportunity to shine light on the other's strengths and contributions and to encourage the growth of his or her positive qualities. Our loved ones and relationships are like flowers that need regular watering to stay fresh and alive. If we do not water the other person's flowers, our love or the relationship may wilt or die.

2. SHARING REGRETS

We may mention any unskillfulness in our actions, speech, or thoughts that we have not yet had an opportunity to apologize for. When we have recognized how we have contributed to the conflict or difficulty, we can apologize right away.

3. EXPRESSING HURT

We may share how we felt hurt by another, due to their actions, speech, or thoughts. Before expressing a hurt, be aware that most of our perceptions are wrong. Often our difficulties and pain originate in the past, in early childhood. By looking deeply we can see that our pain and hurt come from the seeds of suffering within us and not from the other person. You might also ask for a third party that you both trust and respect to be present to hold the space.

4. ASKING FOR SUPPORT

When we share our difficulties with the other person, we help them understand us better. This enables them to offer the kind of support that we really need. We may be currently under a lot of pressure at work or school. We can ask the other person for their understanding and support.

USING A PEACE TREATY

When we get angry, we no longer look like a beautiful flower. We look more like a bomb ready to explode; hundreds of muscles in our face tense up. A "Peace Treaty" is something that individuals, couples, and families can sign in the presence of others to increase the likelihood that we will deal with our anger well. This is not just a piece of paper—it is a practice that can help us live happily together for a long time. The treaty has two parts: one for the person who is angry, and one for the person who has caused the anger. When we get angry or when someone is angry with us, if we follow the terms of the Peace Treaty, we will be guided back to equanimity and we can restore harmony in our relationships.

PEACE TREATY

In Order That We May Live Long and Happily Together, In Order That We May Continually Develop and Deepen Our Love and Understanding, We the Undersigned Vow to Observe and Practice the Following:

I, the one who is angry, agree to:

1 Refrain from saying or doing anything that might cause further damage or escalate the anger.
2 Not suppress my anger.
3 Practice breathing and taking refuge in the island of myself.
4 Calmly, within twenty-four hours, tell the one who has made me angry about my anger and suffering, either verbally or by delivering a Peace Note.
5 Ask for an appointment for later in the week (e.g., Friday evening) to discuss this matter more thoroughly, either verbally or by Peace Note.
6 Not say: "I am not angry. It's okay. I am not suffering. There is nothing to be angry about."
7 Practice breathing and looking deeply into my

daily life—while sitting, lying down, standing, and walking—in order to see:

- a the ways I myself have been unskillful at times.
- b how I have hurt the other person because of my own habit energy.
- c how the strong seed of anger in me is the primary cause of my anger.
- d how the other person's suffering, which waters the seed of my anger, is the secondary cause.
- e how the other person is only seeking relief from his or her own suffering.
- f that as long as the other person suffers, I cannot be truly happy.

8 Apologize immediately, without waiting until the Friday evening, as soon as I realize my unskillfulness and lack of mindfulness.

9 Postpone the Friday meeting if I do not feel calm enough to meet with the other person.

I, the one who has made the other angry, agree to:

1 Respect the other person's feelings, not ridicule him or her, and allow enough time for him or her to calm down.

2 Not press for an immediate discussion.
3 Confirm the other person's request for a meeting, either verbally or by note, and assure him or her that I will be there.
4 Practice breathing and taking refuge in the island of myself to see how:
   a I have seeds of unkindness and anger in me, as well as habit energy, that can make the other person unhappy.
   b I have mistakenly thought that making the other person suffer would relieve my own suffering.
   c By making him or her suffer, I make myself suffer.
5 Apologize as soon as I realize my unskillfulness and lack of mindfulness, without making any attempt to justify myself and without waiting until the Friday meeting.

Signed, ______________________________

The _____ Day of _____________________
in the Year _____ in ___________________

THE PEACE NOTE

If someone has made us angry, we want to let them know about our anger within twenty-four hours. If we feel we're not able to speak to the other person in a calm way and the deadline of twenty-four hours is approaching, we can use a "Peace Note." We don't want to go to sleep without being able to express our emotion in a calm way. This is also good for the other person because they may be wondering why we were not able to smile. The moment we know that the other person has received our note, we already feel some relief. You can use this peace note or create your own to fit the situation.

PEACE NOTE

Date: ______________________

Time: ______________________

Dear ____________________________________,

I wanted to let you know that this morning (afternoon), you said (did) something that made me very angry. I suffered very much. You said (did):

Could we find a time to sit down together and look at this? Could you let me know when would be a good time?

Yours, with love, ______________________________________

HUGGING MEDITATION

Hugging meditation is something to practice with people you love and trust, particularly if you have been upset with each other. To begin, close your eyes, take a deep breath, and visualize yourself and your beloved three hundred years from now. Then, open your arms and hug your loved one. If we can see the impermanent nature of our self and our loved one, we can realize how precious every moment is that we have together. We won't want to waste our time together by being angry and hurting each other.

When you hug someone, first practice breathing in and breathing out to bring to life your insight of impermanence. "Breathing in, I know that life is precious in this moment.

Breathing out, I cherish this moment of life." You smile at the person in front of you, expressing your desire to hold him or her in your arms. This is a practice and a ritual. When you bring your body and mind together to produce your total presence, full of life, it is a ritual. You hold the other person in your arms gently, and breathe in and out three times, cherishing the other person's presence. Then you separate and smile to each other again—a smile of gratitude and love.

LOVE LETTER

If you have difficulties with someone in your life, you might spend some time alone and write a letter to him or her. Give yourself three hours to write a letter using loving speech. While you write the letter, practice looking deeply into the nature of your relationship. Why has communication been difficult? Why has happiness not been possible? You may want to begin like this, “My dear son, I know you have suffered a lot during the past many years. I have not been able to help you—in fact, I have made the situation worse. It is not my intention to make you suffer, my son. Maybe I am not skillful enough. Maybe I try to impose my ideas on you and I make you suffer. In the past I thought you made me suffer, that my suffering was caused by you. Now I realize that I have been responsible for my own suffering, and that I have made you suffer. As your father, I don't want you to suffer." Spend three hours, even a day, writing such a letter. You will find that the person who finishes the letter is not the same person who began it. Peace, understanding, and compassion have transformed you. A miracle can be achieved in twenty-four hours. That is the practice of loving speech.

THE FOURTH MINDFULNESS TRAINING

The Five Mindfulness Trainings are concrete guidelines for the practice of mindfulness, compassion, and understanding. They can help us decide how to respond to situations that arise. The fourth training is about the practice of deep listening and loving speech to restore communication and allow reconciliation to take place.

> Aware of the suffering caused by unmindful speech and the inability to listen to others, I am committed to cultivating loving speech and compassionate listening in order to relieve suffering and to promote reconciliation and peace in myself and among other people, ethnic and religious groups, and nations. Knowing that words can create happiness or suffering, I am committed to speaking truthfully using words

that inspire confidence, joy, and hope. When anger is manifesting in me, I am determined not to speak. I will practice mindful breathing and walking in order to recognize and to look deeply into my anger.

I know that the roots of anger can be found in my wrong perceptions and lack of understanding of the suffering in myself and in the other person. I will speak and listen in a way that can help myself and the other person to transform suffering and see a way out of difficult situations. I am determined not to spread news that I do not know to be certain and not to utter words that can cause division or discord. I will practice Right Diligence to nourish my capacity for understanding, love, joy, and inclusiveness, and gradually transform the anger, violence, and fear that lie deep in my consciousness.

Monastics and visitors practice the art of mindful living in the tradition of Thich Nhat Hanh at our mindfulness practice centers around the world. To reach any of these communities, or for information about how individuals, couples, and families can join in a retreat, please contact:

Plum Village
33580 Dieulivol, France
plumvillage.org

Blue Cliff Monastery
Pine Bush, NY 12566, USA
bluecliffmonastery.org

European Institute of Applied Buddhism
D-51545 Waldbröl, Germany
eiab.eu

Healing Spring Monastery
77510 Verdelot,
France
healingspringmonastery.org

Asian Institute of Applied Buddhism
Ngong Ping, Lantau Island
Hong Kong
pvfhk.org

Mountain Spring Monastery
Bilpin, Victoria 2758
Australia
mountainspringmonastery.org

Magnolia Grove Monastery
Batesville, MS 38606, USA
magnoliagrovemonastery.org

Deer Park Monastery
Escondido, CA 92026, USA
deerparkmonastery.org

Thailand Plum Village
Nakhon Ratchasima
30130 Thailand
thaiplumvillage.org

Maison de l'Inspir
77510 Villeneuve-sur-Bellot
France
maisondelinspir.org

Nhap Luu-Stream Entering Monastery
Porcupine Ridge, Victoria 3461
Australia
nhapluu.org

The Mindfulness Bell, a journal of the art of mindful living in the tradition of Thich Nhat Hanh, is published two times a year by our community. To subscribe or to see the worldwide directory of sanghas (local mindfulness groups), visit **mindfulnessbell.org**.

Parallax Press, a nonprofit publisher founded by Zen Master Thich Nhat Hanh, publishes books and media on the art of mindful living and Engaged Buddhism. We are committed to offering teachings that help transform suffering and injustice. Our aspiration is to contribute to collective insight and awakening, bringing about a more joyful, healthy, and compassionate society.

View our entire library at parallax.org.